The Whispers of the Wind

Kristen Teuta

BookLeaf
Publishing

Presentation by *BookLeaf Publishing*

Web: www.bookleafpub.com

E-mail: info@bookleafpub.com

ISBN: 9789357442213

First edition 2023

To my best friend and my momma.

August

The breeze blows the sounds of dusk through the trees. Pecans and Oaks singing in unison as bats glide under the brewing clouds.

Cicadas, frogs, and other summer creatures create a symphony of evening sounds that cascade from the last light of day into night.

It's undeniable, I am an August child. The sounds resonate through my body and ground my soul almost instantly, bringing on a calming state of nostalgia.

The smell of rain is on the air, so I know my tomatoes will get watered tonight as I pass them by. It can be an unforgiving month.

Gnats in your eyes, mosquitoes eating you alive, sweating from head to toe, ants everywhere you go. But none of that compares to those starry August nights.

Moonlight

Love me like you love the Moon.
Flow through the phases of my emotions,
knowing half of my soul will forever lie in
darkness, dancing amongst the stars.
Brightened by the radiance of the sun,
but not afraid to live in the shadows that emerge.
Forever lonely in the vacuum of space, yet I will
always return, shining to light your way.

Anxiety

Vibrating,
My heart races.
Fingers tingling and
Hands shaking,
So slight.

Jaw unclenches,
 "Breathe....breathe...."
I remember.

I grasp.
I flutter.
My heart stuck in my throat.

Palms hot.
An anxious knowing.
Unknowingly knowingly.

Toes cold,
Feet tingle.
Heart at my tongue.

Thoughts race,
Heart keeps pace.
Both stuck in flight.

Release

They've been there for hours
Welling up behind your eyes and then slowly
fading
Again and again
Sometimes one falls
Ever so slowly
Hoping for invisibility
But it leaves it's trail
A mark of distinction
You casually wipe it away
No one notices
And soon
If starts all over again.

Spiderwebs

It is but a dream
Dripping in feelings lost
Reminders of people forgotten
Soaked with unspoken words.

The words come
Fragments of intelligible thoughts
Cascading through the compartments of my
mind
Scattered from room to room
Like breadcrumbs long forgotten.

Delicate
She is anything but
Your fragile flower.

Kisses of Dawn

Look for me where the sun rises to kiss the
moon,
when morning quietly whispers with the
darkness.

Simple Joy

Walking into work for the day you decide to take
a detour.
You walk past the entrance and continue around
the building.
Searching for that quiet spot, the walkway
alongside the building with little lighting,
hugging a dense thicket of trees and swamp.
A bunny lives in there you recall. Witnessing it
previous mornings before it scampered away at
the realization of your presence.
You walk along, finding the darkest spot on the
path and stare up at the stars.
You know you need to get to work, but in this
moment you seek peace.
Quiet before the day begins, breathing in the
cold air as it nips at your nose and takes over
your fingertips.
You don't mind, this is the coldest morning you
can remember for months and months.
Savoring it you stare up at Orion, distinct in the
darkness of early morning. Breathing in and
absorbing all the sounds of silence. The distant
whirring of cars as others begin their morning
journey.

You take in one last deep breath, pickup the
warm coffee you set on the ground and smile.
You walk around the corner towards the door,
watching the last star as it fades from your
vision, entering the lights of the new day.
You sip that that first sip of coffee and smile as it
cascades through your being.
This is living.

The Slowing

9

Eighth o'clock at night is when my lonely hits.
When I crave connection and warmth from
another person the most. My day has now
slowed enough for me to yearn for comfort from
Reality's sting. Busy as a bee all day until it is
time to lie down for the night and I ache. To be
so close and yet so far from the souls that
heighten your spirit, wondering if there are
thinking of you. Contemplating fleeting nature
of life whilst watching it buzz by and by.

Moments

Warring with words for they can't properly catch
and convey these emotions within.

Peeling away the protective layers until it's just
us, naked minds and flesh.

Waiting for that day I fall asleep in your arms
rather than with my phone in hand.

Breaking Words

It doesn't matter how vicious or well intended, how honest or calm you are in tone, words resonate. They linger and fester, seeping into every part of your mind. Seizing onto every negative thought causing a chain reaction of doubt and shame. They usually remind you of truths you've tried to forget or maybe open your eyes to something you'd not seen within yourself. Truth or projection. Words sting and continue to ring, long after they are spoken.

Bottled

I bottle
I bury
I burst

I lash out
Flayed, naked emotions
Bleeding vulnerability and despair

Anger comes
But can't be satisfied
The problems lie inside

I bottle
I bury
I burst

Every word and look
Like an sting of the yellow jacket
Willing to die to protect

Protect life or protect ego
Consumed by knowing
Your choices are ongoing

Thy own worst enemy
The only one I see
Stares back from mirror
But is it really even me?

Seeking Life

They're are so many distractions. From day one, telling you who to be, what to do, how to look, how to succeed while reminding you that you will surely fail if you don't hot every checkbox of life.

Environment dictates so much working an individual and nature fills in the blanks. Unbalanced, unpredictable, and a different experience for all parties involved. And by this I mean you, human. You are just like the rest of them, grasping for meaning and a definitive plan for life. It's silly when I saw it out loud but it's true.

We are all victims to this consumerist world. Sure, it wasn't always like this, but so quickly and definitely it if and we are here now. Alone with only our technology and ourselves. It's an interesting time. One might argue this had been the case for a decade or two now, but with the recent circumstances of the pandemic, it is now more true than ever.

One's Truth

You are a perfectly imperfect version of your Self. Stay true to you, while growing to greater heights.

Thoughts

Write.
Free your mind of stress before bed
Don't pick fights, but be honest and fair.
Show kindness, even when you don't receive it.
Complain less, be grateful more.
Feed your body and soul properly.
Speak only of yourself, but sparingly.
Water is your best friend accompanied with
coffee.
Don't give up. Don't give in. Don't stop.
Nothing is worth your integrity.
Be bold and observe.
Cleanliness IS godliness. Order is peace.

Mesmerized

Before he can make it to the room I sense him,
smell and feel him with all of my senses.
Intoxicated by every ounce of him.
It has always been that way.
No man has managed to penetrate my barriers,
Letting me free to be wholly myself.
His eyes have always danced with mine,
Trying to tell me a truth I could not yet
comprehend. A knowing that only someone with
his heart could see. His hands are enough to
make any woman swoon. Strong with hard work
etched into their core, yet so delicate in creating
the most intricate designs, sneaking touches and
little pleasures. Slowly and patiently feeding my
desires, while breaking into that wall I fortified
for years. Time and perspective are funny and
absurd concepts. So rarely do they seem to line
up. All you can do is heal and wait. But he, with
those eyes of laughter and hands of delicate
persuasion, is all you couldn't see before and
erases the chaos of life, with his mere presence.
And for that, I am the luckiest person in the
world.

And that, is how I know I'm home.

Tears

I have snot on my sleeve
And tears in my eyes.
I am strong, I'll survive.
Because I know one day
These feelings will die.

do you?

do you feel it?
the longing, the desire
to soak in your essence.
the light you so naturally
Radiate. Joy without effort.

do you hear it?
My Soul aching for yours.
To connect in unison
the world fading away,
worry-free. Love without bounds.

do you see it?
the little things I do
to show you, I love you
the everything you are and will be
Boundless. Love untethered.

Silence

Silences only remind me I can live without.
Words don't flow naturally on paper when the
mind is a whirlpool of thoughts.
Her broken pieces were her most elegant.

Alive

Pain fell from her eyes.
Salty streams flowing down her cheeks.
Cascading off her chin, like raindrops off the
roof in springtime.
Yet she smiled.

She felt alive.

His

His lips curled in a smile
Laughter in his eyes
His face was made for kisses
His heart a treasure, only he could share.

See

Let me see you.
Not your face or eyes
Your lips or smile
Your legs or toes
Your prominent nose.

Let me see you.
Your unmasked soul.

9 789357 442213